What Jesus has to say about living a blessed life

Taught by Pastor Lance Witt

A PURPOSE DRIVEN SMALL GROUP STUDY FROM THE SERMON ON THE MOUNT

PurposeDriven®

Published by PurposeDriven® Publishing.
20 Empire
Lake Forest, CA 92630
www.purposedriven.com

TABLE OF CONTENTS

You are about to embark on a life-changing experience in your small group. Studying God's Word together always impacts our lives in powerful ways. One of the unique features of this curriculum is that it uses God's five purposes for your life as the format for each session. These purposes, as found in *The Purpose Driven Life*, are Fellowship, Discipleship, Ministry, Evangelism, and Worship. When you see the following symbols and elements in the study guide, you will know the particular purpose that section promotes. The format of each session is as follows:

Connect — Intimate connection with God and his family is the foundation for spiritual growth. This section will help you get to know the members of your group. It will also give you the opportunity to check your progress from week to week.

Grow — This section is made up of three components:

1) A weekly Bible memory verse that fits the theme of the session.
2) A weekly video teaching session by Pastor Lance Witt. Follow along using the outline in this study guide.
3) Discussion questions designed to facilitate a deeper understanding of the Bible and to help you consider how the truths of Scripture can impact your life.

Serve — Nothing is more fulfilling than using your God-given gifts to serve the needs of others in God's family. This section will help your group discover how you can serve each other and your church together.

Share — God wants to use your small group to reach your community for Christ. The Share section is designed to give you and your group practical suggestions and exercises for sharing the love of Christ with others.

Worship — In each small group session you will have the opportunity to surrender your hearts to God and express your worship to him. In this section you will be led in various forms of small group worship including prayer, Scripture reading, singing together, and sharing what God is doing in your lives. This portion of your session can be very meaningful for your group.

Host Tips — These brief instructions in gray type are helpful coaching hints for your group host. Here's your first . . .

HOST TIP: THE STUDY GUIDE MATERIAL IS MEANT TO BE YOUR SERVANT, NOT YOUR MASTER. SO PLEASE DON'T FEEL YOU HAVE TO ANSWER EVERY QUESTION IN EVERY SECTION. THE POINT IS NOT TO RACE THROUGH THE SESSION; THE POINT IS TO TAKE TIME TO LET GOD WORK IN YOUR LIVES. NOR IS IT NECESSARY TO "GO AROUND THE CIRCLE" BEFORE YOU MOVE ON TO THE NEXT QUESTION. GIVE PEOPLE THE FREEDOM TO SPEAK, BUT DON'T INSIST THAT THEY DO. YOUR GROUP WILL ENJOY DEEPER, MORE OPEN SHARING AND DISCUSSION IF PEOPLE DON'T FEEL PRESSURED TO SPEAK UP. IF YOUR GROUP IS UNABLE TO WORK THROUGH ALL THE MATERIAL IN A SESSION, WE HAVE RECOMMENDED ONE QUESTION OR ACTIVITY WITH AN ASTERISK (*) IN EACH SECTION OF THE STUDY.

Here is a brief explanation of the features on your small group DVD or VHS. These features include six *Helps for Hosts*, one *Group Lifter*, and six *Video Teaching Sessions*. Here's how they work:

Helps for Hosts are special video messages just for group hosts. They provide brief video instructions from Pastor Lance Witt that will help the host prepare for each week's small group session. The group host should watch these features before the group arrives for each study.

The *Group Lifter* is an introductory message to your whole group from Pastor Lance Witt. Be sure to show this *Group Lifter* to your group before you watch the video teaching for session one.

The *Video Teaching Sessions* provide your group with the teaching for each week of the study. Watch these features with your group. After watching the video teaching, continue in your study by working through the discussion questions and activities in the study guide.

Follow these simple steps for a successful small group session:

1. Hosts: Before your group arrives, watch the "Helps for Hosts" feature by Pastor Lance Witt. This brief video message will help you prepare for your small group session.

2. Group: Open your group meeting by using the Connect section in your study guide.

3. Group: Watch Pastor Lance's video teaching and follow along in the outlines in the study guide.

4. Group: Complete the rest of the discussion materials for each session in the study guide.

It's just that simple. Have a great study together!

SESSION ONE
MATTHEW 5:1–3

Connect . . . . .15 minutes

HOST TIP: IF YOUR GROUP IS UNABLE TO WORK THROUGH THE ENTIRE CURRICULUM, WE HAVE RECOMMENDED ONE QUESTION OR ACTIVITY WITH AN ASTERISK (*) IN EACH SECTION OF THE STUDY.

*1. Give everyone a chance to introduce themselves and share how they came to be part of this group.

2. Open to the *Purpose Driven Group Guidelines* in the *Small Group Resources* section of your study guide, page 62. Take a few minutes to review these group guidelines before you begin this study. These guidelines will help everyone know what to expect and how to contribute to a meaningful small group time.

3. Who is the happiest person you know? Why do you think they are so happy?

Grow . . . . .45 minutes

Key Verse

". . . I have come that they may have life, and have it to the full."
John 10:10b (NIV)

Watch the video lesson now and follow along in your outline.

"I denied myself nothing my eyes desired; I refused my heart no pleasure. My heart took delight in all my work, and this was the reward for all my labor. Yet when I surveyed all that my hands had done and what I had toiled to achieve, everything was meaningless, a chasing after the wind; nothing was gained under the sun." Ecclesiastes 2:10–11 (NIV)

". . . I have come that they may have life, and have it to the full." John 10:10 (NIV)

By-Products of External Religion

1. You become known for what you are _____ .

2. You develop an _____ .

3. You develop a _____ attitude.

Jesus had a different kind of righteousness in mind, an _____

_____ .

"My kingdom is not of this world." John 18:36a (NIV)

Blessed are the Poor in Spirit . . .

"Now when he saw the crowds, he went up on a mountainside and sat down. His disciples came to him, and he began to teach them saying: Blessed are the poor in spirit, for theirs is the kingdom of heaven." Matthew 5:1–3 (NIV)

What does it mean to be poor in spirit?

- Having a proper understanding of your _____ in relationship to God.

- Acknowledging my _____ .

- It's the fundamental characteristic of a person who is going to live a

  _____ .

  ". . . all our righteous acts are like filthy rags . . ." Isaiah 64:6 (NIV)

- The recognition that I am spiritually bankrupt and in _____

  _____ .

- This first Beatitude is about a deep sense of _____ .

Discussion Questions

1. Before you became a Christian, did you view Christianity as "rules-keeping?" What are some of the things we rely on for our own sense of righteousness instead of God's mercy and grace?

2. When you came to Christ, how keen was your sense of "spiritual bankruptcy?" How important is it for people who are considering the gospel to be aware of their spiritual bankruptcy?

*3. The concept of the kingdom of God is central to the Sermon on the Mount. What does it mean to live in the kingdom of God here and now? How does kingdom living relate to happiness?

4. Pastor Lance said that for many people in church, "the gospel often seems more like an offer for repair and remodel rather than regeneration." Discuss the difference between remodel and regeneration.

> **HOST TIP:** DEPENDING ON THE SIZE OF YOUR GROUP, TIME AVAILABILITY, OR STAGE OF MATURITY, ADDITIONAL STUDY QUESTIONS ARE PROVIDED NEAR THE END OF THIS LESSON FOR YOUR GROUP TO STUDY. YOU MAY WANT TO USE THESE QUESTIONS AS SUGGESTED HOMEWORK EACH WEEK OR TURN THERE NOW FOR EXTENDED DISCUSSION.

Serve . . . .**10 minutes**

*1. Discuss how God can use your experiences of brokenness and spiritual bankruptcy to minister to the needs of others.

Share . . . .**10 minutes**

*1. How has rules-based religion affected the attitudes of unchurched people toward Christians?

2. It has been said that a Christian leading someone to Christ is like one beggar showing another beggar where the food is. In light of this, how does being poor in spirit fit in with telling your friends about Jesus?

Worship . . . . .10 minutes

HOST TIP: TO MAXIMIZE PRAYER TIME AND ALLOW GREATER OPPORTUNITY FOR PERSONAL SHARING, BREAK INTO SUBGROUPS OF THREE OR FOUR PEOPLE. THIS IS ESPECIALLY IMPORTANT IF YOUR GROUP HAS MORE THAN EIGHT MEMBERS.

1. Nearly everyone is familiar with the old hymn, "Amazing Grace." If you are comfortable singing together, sing the hymn (words below). If not, have someone read through the lyrics while everyone follows along.

Amazing Grace

John Newton

Amazing grace! How sweet the sound
That saved a wretch like me!
I once was lost, but now am found;
Was blind, but now I see.

'Twas grace that taught my heart to fear,
And grace my fears relieved;
How precious did that grace appear
The hour I first believed.

Through many dangers, toils, and snares
I have already come.
'Tis grace hath brought me safe thus far,
And grace will lead me home.

When we've been there ten thousand years,
Bright shining as the sun,
We've no less days to sing God's praise
Than when we'd first begun.

*2. Move right into a time of prayer directed at admitting your needs/sins before God and thanking him for his forgiveness and grace.

3. Close your time by praying for any needs in your group. Record your group's prayer requests on the *Small Group Prayer and Praise Report* in the *Small Group Resources* section on page 65. Keeping track of group prayer requests and answers to prayer would be a great job for someone in your group. Any volunteers?

Before You Leave

1. Take a few minutes to look at the *Small Group Calendar* in the *Small Group Resources* section, page 67 of this study guide. Healthy groups share responsibilities and group ownership. Fill out the calendar together, noting where you will meet each week, who will facilitate your discussion time, and who will provide a meal or snack. Note special events, such as birthdays, anniversaries, socials, etc. Coordinating these details would be another great job for someone in the group.

2. Collect phone numbers and email addresses from your small group members. The group roster (called *My Small Group*) on the inside front cover of your study guide is a good place to keep this information. Pass your study guides around the circle and have your group members fill in their contact information.

Additional Study

The Kingdom of God was the central theme of the preaching of Jesus Christ. It is a phrase used more than fifty times in the gospels. (In Matthew the phrase "Kingdom of Heaven" is used in its place.) It expresses both an abstract idea of God's rule today and a concrete idea of God's rule in the age to come.

1. Read Matthew 3:2. What did John the Baptist mean when he said "The kingdom of heaven is near?" How did he tell the people to respond to this news? What does it mean to repent?

2. In Matthew 4:17 (NKJV), Jesus says, "Repent, for the kingdom of heaven is at hand." What is the significance of the phrase, "at hand?"

3. How does the Sermon on the Mount relate to the Kingdom of God?

Preparation for Next Time

Use the *Daily Quiet Time Verses* at the back of this booklet and record any thoughts or direction you receive from the Lord. We suggest you use a quiet time journal to record your thoughts.

Read Matthew 5:4–5 in preparation for your next session.

SESSION TWO
MATTHEW 5:4–5

Connect . . . . .10 minutes

> **HOST TIP:** IF YOUR GROUP IS UNABLE TO WORK THROUGH THE ENTIRE CURRICULUM, WE HAVE RECOMMENDED ONE QUESTION OR ACTIVITY WITH AN ASTERISK (*) IN EACH SECTION OF THE STUDY.

*1. Welcome any people who are new to your group.

2. Complete the sentence, "Happiness is . . ." Don't think too much about this and don't grasp for correct "spiritual" answers. Use real things like baseball or a sunset, and use this as an opportunity to get to know each other's likes and dislikes.

Grow . . . . .40 minutes

Key Verse

*"When he comes, he will convict the world of guilt
in regard to sin and righteousness and judgment."*
John 16:8 (NIV)

 Watch the video lesson now and follow along in your outline.

" . . . when Jesus saw the huge crowds beginning to follow him, he withdrew to the mountainside. . ." Matthew 5:1

Blessed are those who mourn . . .

"Blessed are those who mourn, for they will be comforted." Matthew 5:4 (NIV)

- True happiness begins with acknowledging the darkness of our own

  sin and then responding with _____ and

  _____ .

  "When he comes, he will convict the world of guilt in regard to sin and righteousness and judgment." John 16:8 (NIV)

- Comfort comes in knowing that God _____ my sin.

- You cannot fully appreciate the wonder of your salvation without

  appreciating what you have been _____ .

Blessed are the meek . . .

"Blessed are the meek, for they will inherit the earth." Matthew 5:5 (NIV)

- Meekness is power under _____.

  "...for I am meek and lowly in heart ..." Matthew 11:29 (KJV)

  "...for I am gentle and humble in heart ..." Matthew 11:29 (NIV)

- Being meek means that I no longer live for my _____.

- As the children of God, the death of Christ means an _____ is coming our way.

Discussion Questions

> **HOST TIP:** IF YOUR GROUP HAS EIGHT OR MORE MEMBERS, WE SUGGEST YOU BREAK INTO SUBGROUPS OF THREE OR FOUR PEOPLE FOR GREATER PARTICIPATION AND DEEPER DISCUSSION. AT THE END OF THE DISCUSSION TIME, COME BACK TOGETHER AND HAVE SOMEONE FROM EACH GROUP REPORT ON THE HIGHLIGHTS OF THEIR DISCUSSIONS.

1. How does the truth that we all have a sin-nature strike you? Do you have a hard time accepting this?

2. How does this second Beatitude, "Blessed are those who mourn," relate to the first Beatitude we discussed last week, "Blessed are the poor in spirit?"

3. What biblical examples of "power under control" did Pastor Lance share? Who else can you think of in scripture who also demonstrated meekness?

*4. If it's really true that "the meek are blessed," how should this truth impact the way you live today?

HOST TIP: DEPENDING ON THE SIZE OF YOUR GROUP, TIME AVAILABILITY, OR STAGE OF MATURITY, ADDITIONAL STUDY QUESTIONS ARE PROVIDED NEAR THE END OF THIS LESSON FOR YOUR GROUP TO STUDY. YOU MAY WANT TO USE THESE QUESTIONS AS SUGGESTED HOMEWORK EACH WEEK OR TURN THERE RIGHT NOW FOR EXTENDED DISCUSSION.

Serve . . . . .15 minutes

*1. How can you put meekness into practice by serving someone this week?

2. Optional: Write a note or email of encouragement this week to someone who exemplifies gentleness to you.

Share . . . . .10 minutes

*1. How can gentleness be an effective evangelism tool?

2. Think of ways in which you individually and as a small group can demonstrate true meekness by serving people in your community.

♥ Worship ....15 minutes

*1. Break into subgroups of three or four people and pray for each other about this question: Is there an area of your life you need to "willfully surrender" to God? This could be a relationship, a hope, a habit, a grudge, or something you feel you have a right to hold on to.

2. If you thought of someone during the Share section of this study, tell their name to the group and pray for that person.

Before You Leave

1. Turn to the *Small Group Calendar* on page 67 of your study guide. Pick a date and time when your group can get together for a ministry or mission project, such as volunteering at a soup-kitchen, helping a shut-in with home repairs or yard work, or taking on a project at your church.

2. Was anyone missing from your group this week? If someone was absent, ask for a volunteer from the group to call or email that person and let them know they were missed. It's very important for people to know they are cared about.

Additional Study

Study 1 John 1:5–7 (NLT)

"This is the message he has given us to announce to you: God is light and there is no darkness in him at all. So we are lying if we say we have fellowship with God but go on living in spiritual darkness. We are not living in the truth. But if we are living in the light of God's presence, just as Christ is, then we have fellowship with each other, and the blood of Jesus, his Son, cleanses us from every sin."

1. Pastor Lance talked about the shirt he could only wear in dark rooms because of the spot on it. This is what John means about walking in spiritual darkness. It's not telling the whole truth about ourselves. What are ways in which we try to hide our sinfulness and avoid the light?

2. What happens when we come into the light together? How can we create an atmosphere in our group where we can do this better?

Preparation for Next Time

1. Use the *Daily Quiet Time Verses* at the back of this booklet and record any thoughts or direction you receive from the Lord. We suggest you use a quiet time journal to record your thoughts.

2. Read Matthew 5:6–7 and write down your deepest desires. What do you hunger for?

SESSION THREE
MATTHEW 5:6–7

Connect . . . . .10 minutes

HOST TIP: IF YOUR GROUP IS UNABLE TO WORK THROUGH THE ENTIRE CURRICULUM, WE HAVE RECOMMENDED ONE QUESTION OR ACTIVITY WITH AN ASTERISK (*) IN EACH SECTION OF THE STUDY.

*1. Memorizing scripture is a challenge for all of us, yet it is a wonderful spiritual habit. Pair up with one other person and try to memorize this week's Key Verse. How is this verse an encouragement to you?

Grow . . . . .40 minutes

Key Verse

*"God made him who had no sin to be sin for us,
so that in him we might become the righteousness of God."*
2 Corinthians 5:21 (NIV)

Watch the video lesson now and follow along in your outline.

Blessed are those who hunger and thirst for righteousness . . .

"Blessed are those who hunger and thirst for righteousness, for they will be filled." Matthew 5:6 (NIV)

". . . you fool. This very night your life will be demanded from you . . . this is how it will be with anyone who stores up things for himself but is not rich toward God." Luke 12:20–21 (NIV)

- What Jesus condemns is an appetite and hunger that is for the stuff of this world rather than for _____.

Two Meanings of Righteousness

"God made him who had no sin to be sin for us, so that in him we might become the righteousness of God." 2 Corinthians 5:21 (NIV)

- If you have received Christ as _____, you are righteous.
- This beatitude is about fueling our _____ for that process of becoming like Jesus.

"O God, you are my God, earnestly I seek you; my soul thirsts for you, my body longs for you, in a dry and weary land where there is no water." Psalm 63:1 (NIV)

"But whatever was to my profit I now consider loss for the sake of Christ. What is more, I consider everything a loss compared to the surpassing greatness of knowing Christ Jesus my Lord, for whose sake I have lost all things. I consider them rubbish that I may gain Christ." Philippians 3:7–8 (NIV)

Blessed are the merciful . . .

"Blessed are the merciful, for they will be shown mercy." Matthew 5:7 (NIV)

- _____ is getting what you don't deserve.

  _____ is not getting what you do deserve.

  > *"Because of the Lord's great love we are not consumed, for his compassions never fail."* Lamentations 3:22 (NIV)

- The expression of mercy toward others in our lives is the

  _____ of the mercy that we have personally received.

- Happiness comes in dishing out large doses of _____ .

Discussion Questions

1. What does it mean to "hunger and thirst" for righteousness? What does that look like in your life?

*2. When we trust Jesus Christ as our Savior, we are immediately made righteous in God's eyes. What does that mean?

3. Who do you know that exhibits a deep passion and hunger for Christ? How does that person demonstrate their passion?

4. Grace is getting what you don't deserve. Mercy is not getting what you do deserve. Share about a time when someone showed you grace or mercy. How did it make you feel?

 Serve . . . .**10 minutes**

1. Share with the group a situation or the name of a person to whom you could show grace or mercy this week. How will you do it? What difference could it make in their life? What difference could it make in yours?

_____

_____

 Share . . . .**20 minutes**

1. Think of a specific instance when God was gracious or merciful to you. Your story can be a great way to share your faith with non-believers. Break into subgroups of two or three people and practice telling your stories to each other. Each person should take no more than three or four minutes so that everyone will have a chance to share their stories.

Worship . . . . .10 minutes

> **HOST TIP:** TO MAXIMIZE PRAYER TIME AND ALLOW GREATER OPPORTUNITY FOR PERSONAL SHARING, BREAK INTO SUBGROUPS OF THREE OR FOUR PEOPLE. THIS IS ESPECIALLY IMPORTANT IF YOUR GROUP HAS MORE THAN EIGHT MEMBERS.

*1. Offer prayers of thanksgiving to God for specific acts of grace and mercy in your life.

2. As a believer, is there anything in your life that is distracting you from being a passionate follower of Christ? It could be a relationship, a goal, a hobby, or a fear of some kind. If so, confess it to the Lord, and ask him to help you reprioritize your life.

3. In your discussion of people to whom you need to show grace or mercy, undoubtedly some very challenging relationships came to mind. Pray specifically for people in your group who are finding it difficult to be gracious or merciful toward someone else.

Before You Leave

1. Turn to the *Small Group Calendar* on page 67 of your study guide. Pick a date and time when your group can get together for some kind of social outing: a group family barbecue or picnic, a ball game, a girls' night out, a guys' night out, etc.

Additional Study

1. Read 2 Corinthians 5:20–21. Discuss the "great exchange" that happens as the result of our salvation. Being righteous (in Christ) is one thing; living a righteous life is another. How should the knowledge of our righteousness in Christ translate into righteous living?

2. Read the parable of the unmerciful servant in Matthew 17:23–35. How could a man who had been forgiven so much, refuse to show mercy to someone who owed him so little? According to this parable, why should we show mercy to others?

3. Talk about the relationship between righteousness and mercy, as seen in Matthew 5:6–7.

Preparation for Next Time

1. Use the *Daily Quiet Time Verses* at the back of this booklet and record any thoughts or direction you receive from the Lord. We suggest you use a quiet time journal to record your thoughts.

2. Read Matthew 5:8–9 in preparation for your next session, and think about this: There is a common tenet that says, "See no evil; hear no evil; speak no evil." In many circles this has been attributed erroneously as a Christian saying. It is not. But it raises a question: If you could remove all outside evil influences, could you live a pure life?

SESSION FOUR
MATTHEW 5:8–9

Connect . . . . .15 minutes

> HOST TIP: IF YOUR GROUP IS UNABLE TO WORK THROUGH THE ENTIRE CURRICULUM, WE HAVE RECOMMENDED ONE
> QUESTION OR ACTIVITY WITH AN ASTERISK (*) IN EACH SECTION OF THE STUDY.

*1. We are now half-way through the first volume of our study on *Inside Out Living*. How is God using this study to help you grow?

2. Did anyone follow-up on your commitment from our last session to reach out to someone with grace and mercy this week? How did it go?

3. Many things look beautiful on the outside but are bad on the inside, such as a poisonous flower or a rotten egg. Other things are unattractive on the outside but beautiful on the inside, such as a kiwi fruit or a geode rock. What are some other examples? What does this observation from nature tell us about people?

Grow . . . . .45 minutes

Key Verse

*"Love the Lord your God with all your heart and
with all your soul and with all your mind."*
Matthew 22:37 (NIV)

Watch the video lesson now and follow along in your outline.

Blessed are the pure in heart . . .

"Blessed are the pure in heart, for they will see God." Matthew 5:8 (NIV)

• If you want to have a fulfilled life, you have to do a scan of your

_____ .

> *"Above all else, guard your heart, for it is the wellspring of life."*
> Proverbs 4:23 (NIV)

• Loving God is first and foremost a matter of your _____

and _____ , not just your actions and behaviors.

• When you do something with _____ , God is
pleased and you are a success.

• Purity of heart brings God into _____ .

Blessed are the peacemakers . . .

"Blessed are the peacemakers, for they will be called sons of God."
Matthew 5:9 (NIV)

• When Jesus talks about peacemaking, he means actively bringing

 people _____ who are estranged.

Three ways that we can be peacemakers:

• Be _____ to God personally.

 "For God was pleased to have all his fullness dwell in him, and through
 him to reconcile to himself all things, whether things on earth or things
 in heaven, by making peace through his blood, shed on the cross."
 Colossians 1:19–20 (NIV)

• _____ others to the peace that God offers.

 "All this is from God who reconciled us to himself through Christ and
 gave us the ministry of reconciliation: that God was reconciling the
 world to himself in Christ, not counting men's sins against them. And
 he has committed to us the message of reconciliation. We are therefore
 Christ's ambassadors, as though God were making his appeal through
 us." 2 Corinthians 5:18–20 (NIV)

• Bring _____ between people.

"If it is possible, as far as it depends on you, live at peace with everyone." Romans 12:18 (NIV)

Discussion Questions

*1. The Bible teaches in 1 Samuel 16:7 that *"man looks at the outward appearance, but the Lord looks at the heart."* And Jesus warned in Matthew 15:8 about people who *"honor me with their lips, but their hearts are far from me."* How do those truths impact you? Why do you think God places so much emphasis on the heart?

2. How can you measure the condition of your heart to see if it is "pure?" What does your answer tell you about judging the hearts of others?

3. Jesus said the pure in heart will see God. What do you think it means to "see" God? Is that just for the "after-life," or is there a present application to this truth?

4. According to 2 Corinthians 5:20, we are "ambassadors" of Christ's peace. What does that mean to you, and how can you represent the peace of Christ to the world?

Serve . . . .**15 minutes**

1. A spiritual partner can help keep you on track in your spiritual growth. Take a moment to pair up with someone in your group who can be your partner for the remainder of this study. Please have men partner with men, and women partner with women.

*2. Now discuss the following question with your spiritual partner: Pastor Lance quoted someone as saying, "Peace is that glorious moment when everyone stops to reload." Are you currently at war with someone? If so, write their name on the line below:

_____

3. Make a commitment to your spiritual partner that you will contact the person whose name you wrote if at all possible this week and at least do your part to make peace. Share with your partner the difficulties and barriers you anticipate in this encounter, and then pray for each other that God will give you the courage to take the right step.

 Share . . . .**10 minutes**

*While still with your spiritual partner, write the name of someone you know who is not at peace with God:

_____
Name

Talk with your partner about how you might help this person take a step closer to God. Then briefly pray for each other and for the person you have in mind. Ask God to show you how to bring them closer to peace with him.

Worship . . . . .5 minutes

1. Pray aloud together the Peace Prayer by St. Francis of Assisi:

   Lord, make me an instrument of your peace.
   Where there is hatred, let me sow love;
   Where there is injury, pardon;
   Where there is doubt, faith;
   Where there is despair, hope;
   Where there is darkness, light;
   Where there is sadness, joy.
   O divine Master,
   Grant that I may not so much seek to be consoled
   As to console;
   To be understood, as to understand;
   To be loved, as to love.
   For it is in giving that we receive;
   It is in pardoning that we are pardoned;
   And it is in dying that we are born to eternal life.
   Amen.

*2. Close your time by praying for any needs in your group. Record your group's prayer requests on the *Small Group Prayer and Praise Report* in the *Small Group Resources* section on page 65.

Additional Study

In 1 Corinthians 4:3–5 (NIV), Paul comments on conscience and judging:

"I care very little if I am judged by you or by any human court; indeed, I do not even judge myself. My conscience is clear, but that does not make me innocent. It is the Lord who judges me. Therefore judge nothing before the appointed time; wait until the Lord comes. He will bring to light what is hidden in darkness and will expose the motives of men's hearts. At that time each will receive his praise from God."

1. According to this passage, can we judge our own motives? How about the motives of others?

2. According to verse 4, what does a clear conscience do for you? What does it not do?

3. What would you like the Lord to find in your heart when he comes?

Preparation for Next Time

1. Read Matthew 5:10–12 and pray for Christians who are being persecuted in other parts of the world.

2. Use the *Daily Quiet Time Verses* at the back of this booklet and record any thoughts or direction you receive from the Lord. We suggest you use a quiet time journal to record your thoughts.

SESSION FIVE
MATTHEW 5:10–12

Connect . . . . .15 minutes

HOST TIP: IF YOUR GROUP IS UNABLE TO WORK THROUGH THE ENTIRE CURRICULUM, WE HAVE RECOMMENDED ONE QUESTION OR ACTIVITY WITH AN ASTERISK (*) IN EACH SECTION OF THE STUDY.

1. In our last session we were challenged to reach out to someone with whom we have a broken or strained relationship. Were you able to follow-up on your commitment? Would anyone like to share their "peace-making" experience with the group?

*2. Would anyone like to share a praise report for an answer to prayer?

3. What is one area where you have grown spiritually in the last year?

Grow . . . . .45 minutes

Key Verse

"In fact, everyone who wants to live a godly life
in Christ Jesus will be persecuted."
2 Timothy 3:12 (NIV)

Watch the video lesson now and follow along in your outline.

Blessed are those who are persecuted because of their righteousness . . .

"Blessed are those who are persecuted because of righteousness, for theirs is the kingdom of heaven. Blessed are you when people insult you, persecute you and falsely say all kinds of evil against you because of me. Rejoice and be glad, because great is your reward in heaven, for in the same way they persecuted the prophets who were before you." Matthew 5:10–12 (NIV)

- As you live like Jesus you too can expect some _____ and

  _____ along the way.

"If the world hates you, keep in mind that it hated me first. If you belonged to the world, it would love you as its own. As it is, you do not belong to the world, but I have chosen you out of the world. That is why the world hates you. Remember the words I spoke to you: 'no servant is greater than his master.' If they persecuted me, they will persecute you also." John 15:18–20 (NIV)

- There is no honor in being persecuted because you are

  _____ , _____ , and _____ .

"If you suffer, it should not be as a murderer or thief or any other kind of criminal, or even as a meddler. However, if you suffer as a Christian, do not be ashamed, but praise God that you bear that name." 1 Peter 4:15–16 (NIV)

"The apostles left the Sanhedrin, rejoicing because they had been counted worthy of suffering disgrace for the Name." Acts 5:41 (NIV)

Promises attached to this Beatitude

1. _____ , ". . . for theirs is the kingdom of heaven."

2. _____ , ". . . great is your reward in heaven . . ."

3. _____ , ". . . in the same way they persecuted the prophets who were before you."

"Some faced jeers and flogging, while still others were chained and put in prison. They were stoned; they were sawed in two; they were put to death by the sword. They went about in sheepskins and goatskins, destitute, persecuted, and mistreated—the world was not worthy of them."
Hebrews 11:36–38a (NIV)

Discussion Questions

1. In your opinion, why does the world hate Christians?

2. In the history of the church, persecution has been the norm, not the exception. Today in our country, in what ways are we likely to experience rejection or persecution?

*3. Have you ever been insulted, persecuted, or falsely accused because of your faith? How did you react? How do you feel now about that experience and the way you responded to it? What did you learn through it all?

4. Jesus tells us to "rejoice and be glad" whenever we are criticized or persecuted for our faith. What do you think about that? Is it an unrealistic expectation?

Serve . . . . .10 minutes

1. Is anyone in your group currently being persecuted or maligned for being a Christian? How can the rest of your group support and encourage your group members who are suffering in this way?

Share . . . . .10 minutes

1. What is the difference between being bold with your faith and being obnoxious?

*2. Sometimes we are persecuted because of the poor behavior of other Christians. How can you change a bad impression left by another Christian's insensitivity or misbehavior?

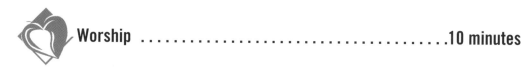

Worship . . . . .10 minutes

1. In your prayer time together, take a few moments to think of specific, personal ways in which God has shown his love to you. Then offer prayers of thanksgiving for God's love.

*2. Take some time to pray for any members of your group who are being maligned or mistreated for their faith. Pray that God will give them courage and strength. Then pray for persecuted Christians around the world.

3. Close your time by praying for any needs in your group. Record your group's prayer requests on the *Small Group Prayer and Praise Report* in the *Small Group Resources* section on page 65.

Before You Leave

1. There is just one session left in this volume of our study on the Sermon on the Mount. We hope you will continue with the next volume, titled *"Inside Out Living — What Jesus has to say about living beyond yourself."* Take a few minutes to discuss your thoughts about the future of your small group. Do you want to keep meeting together? (We hope you will!) Are there any changes you would like to make, such as your meeting place, date and time of your meetings, changes in responsibilities, etc.? Talk about these things and address any concerns that might be raised.

2. It's time for a party! Start making plans now for a group celebration or meal together. This should be a time just to focus on fellowship. Get out your calendars and decide on a date and location. And be sure to decide what kind of food you will have—it could be a gourmet meal, a potluck, a picnic, or just a call-out for pizza.

Additional Study

1 Peter 3:15 (NIV) says: *"But in your hearts set apart Christ as Lord. Always be prepared to give an answer to everyone who asks you to give the reason for the hope that you have. But do this with gentleness and respect."*

1. Break this verse into separate phrases. What does each phrase teach you about sharing your faith with others?

2. How would someone know to ask you about the hope you have?

Preparation for Next Time

1. Read Matthew 5:11–16.

2. As you listen to the news or read the paper this week, look for references to Christians. Do they have a positive or negative influence?

3. Use the *Daily Quiet Time Verses* at the back of this booklet and record any thoughts or direction you receive from the Lord. We suggest you use a quiet time journal to record your thoughts.

SESSION SIX
MATTHEW 5:13–16

Connect . . . . .10 minutes

*1. Today's study is all about influence. Who has had a profound influence on your life? In what way did they influence you?

2. What is one principle, application, or idea you have been working on as a result of this study? Share how you are planning to put that principle, application, or idea to work in your life on a daily basis.

Grow . . . . .40 minutes

Key Verse

"In the same way, let your light shine before men, that they may see your good deeds and praise your Father in heaven."
Matthew 5:16 (NIV)

Watch the video lesson now and follow along in your outline.

Attitudes of Christians

- _____ — These are people who have adopted the attitude, "Go along to get along."

- _____ — These are believers who work very hard to separate themselves from the world.

- _____ — These are believers who are having a positive influence for Christ.

"You are the salt of the earth. But if the salt loses its saltiness, how can it be made salty again? It is no longer good for anything, except to be thrown out and trampled by men. You are the light of the world. A city on a hill cannot be hidden. Neither do people light a lamp and put it under a bowl. Instead they put it on its stand, and it gives light to everyone in the house. In the same way, let your light shine before men, that they may see your good deeds and praise your Father in heaven."
Matthew 5:13–16 (NIV)

Steps to Becoming a Person of Spiritual Influence

- Understand the _____ of your mission.

- Rub shoulders with those you are called to _____ .

"While Jesus was having dinner at Matthew's house, many tax collectors and 'sinners' came and ate with him and his disciples. When the Pharisees saw this, they asked his disciples, 'Why does your teacher eat with tax collectors and "sinners"?' On hearing this, Jesus said, 'It is not the healthy who need a doctor, but the sick.'" Matthew 9:10–12 (NIV)

• Maintain your _____ .

• Accept that you are God's _____ .

• Live your faith _____ .

"Go out into the world uncorrupted, a breath of fresh air in this squalid and polluted society. Provide people with a glimpse of good living and of the living God. Carry the light-giving Message into the night."
Philippians 2:15 (Msg)

Discussion Questions

1. How often do you "rub shoulders" with the world. Do you think you are rubbing off on them, or are they rubbing off on you? Who is having the greater influence?

2. How can you be more proactive and intentional about increasing your influence in the world around you?

*3. Pastor Lance says: "God has an assignment for you. He has a mission in the world he wants you to fulfill." What might your mission be?

4. How effective is your church at influencing your community for Christ?

Serve . . . . .15 minutes

*Your group is called to use its influence to serve your church and to serve the world. What can your group do together to be salt and light in your church and in your community? Take a few minutes to plan a group project.

Share . . . . .20 minutes

*Break into groups of 3 or 4 and practice telling your stories to each other of how you came to Christ. Since we usually don't tell our stories unsolicited, assume that you have just been asked one of the following questions. Pick any question you would like to respond to or make up your own. Be clear and concise, and don't use "churchy" words.

- "Oh, are you one of those born-again Christians? Why do you believe that stuff?"

- "Hey, did you just use a cuss word? And I thought you were a Christian!"

- "How can you manage to hang tough after all you've been through?"

Worship ....10 minutes

> **HOST TIP:** To MAXIMIZE PRAYER TIME AND ALLOW GREATER OPPORTUNITY FOR PERSONAL SHARING, BREAK INTO SUBGROUPS OF THREE OR FOUR PEOPLE. THIS IS ESPECIALLY IMPORTANT IF YOUR GROUP HAS MORE THAN EIGHT MEMBERS.

1. Is there some area of your life where the salt of your influence has lost its saltiness? It could be in a friendship, your work environment, or even in your own home. Search your heart and ask God where you might be losing the edge on your personal testimony. Then pray for each other that God will help you to be a stronger influence in the world.

*2. Use the rest of your time for prayer and praise about what you have learned in your small group. What changes have been brought about in your life since you started coming? Take a few minutes to share a word of praise, and then offer prayers of thankfulness to God for what he has done in and through your group.

Before You Leave

1. If you haven't already done so, take some time now to talk about your future together as a small group. Where will you go from here? If you plan to continue meeting together, when and where will you meet? What will you study? Is there anything you want to do differently in your group life?

2. We encourage you to have a party or picnic together—a time to focus on fellowship and celebrate what God has done throughout the last several weeks. This gathering is also a good opportunity to bring friends who might want to join your small group. It gives potential group members a nonthreatening environment in which to get acquainted with the rest of you. Talk about this with your group: Set a date, time, and location, and decide what kind of food you will have.

Additional Study

Write down the name of a person you admire who in your estimation is having a positive influence for Christ in the world.

_____

What qualities does this person have?

_____

_____

How are they being "salt?"

_____

_____

How are they being "light?"

_____

_____

SMALL GROUP RESOURCES

Helps for Hosts
Top Ten Ideas for New Hosts

Congratulations! As the Host of your small group, you have responded to the call to help shepherd Jesus' flock. Few other tasks in the family of God surpass the contribution you will be making.

On the curriculum videotape or DVD, you will find Helps for Hosts that offer insights and coaching for facilitating each week's session. Each Helps for Hosts feature is taught by Pastor Lance Witt and is 3–5 minutes long.

As you prepare to facilitate your group, whether it is one session or the entire series, here are a few additional thoughts to keep in mind. We encourage you to read and review these tips with each new discussion host before he or she leads.

Remember you are not alone. God knows everything about you, and he knew you would be asked to facilitate your group. Even though you may not feel ready, this is common for all good hosts. God promises, *"I will never leave you; I will never abandon you"* (Hebrews 13:5 TEV). Whether you are facilitating for one evening, several weeks, or a lifetime, you will be blessed as you serve.

1. **Don't try to do it alone.** Pray right now for God to help you build a healthy team. If you can enlist a co-host to help you shepherd the group, you will find your experience much richer. This is your chance to involve as many people as you can in building a healthy group. All you have to do is ask people to help. You'll be surprised at the response.

2. **Be friendly and be yourself.** God wants to use your unique gifts and temperament. Be sure to greet people at the door with a big smile . . . this can set the mood for the whole gathering. Remember, they are taking as big a step as you are to show up at your house! Don't try to do things exactly like another host; do them in a way that fits you. Admit when you don't have an answer and apologize when you make a mistake. Your group will love you for it and you'll sleep better at night.

3. **Prepare for your meeting ahead of time.** Review the session and the video Helps for Hosts. Write down your responses to each question. Pay special attention to exercises that ask group members to do something other than engage in discussion. These exercises will help your group live what the Bible teaches, not just talk about it. Be sure you understand how an exercise works. If the exercise employs one of the items in the *Small Group Resource* section (such as the *Group Guidelines*), be sure to look over that item so you'll know how it works.

4. **Pray for your group members by name.** Before you begin your session, take a few moments and pray for each member by name. You may want to review the prayer list at least once a week. Ask God to use your time together to touch the heart of every person in your group. Expect God to lead you to whomever he wants you to encourage or challenge in a special way. If you listen, God will surely lead.

5. **When you ask a question, be patient.** Someone will eventually respond. Sometimes people need a moment or two of silence to think about the question. If silence doesn't bother you, it won't bother anyone else. After someone responds, affirm the response with a simple "thanks" or "great answer." Then ask, "How about somebody else?" or "Would someone who hasn't shared like to add anything?" Be sensitive to new people or reluctant members who aren't ready to say, pray, or do anything. If you give them a safe setting, they will blossom over time. If someone in your group is a "wall flower" who sits silently through every session, consider talking to them privately and encouraging them to participate. Let them know how important they are to you—that they are loved and appreciated, and that the group would value their input. Remember, still water often runs deep.

6. **Provide transitions between questions.** Ask if anyone would like to read the paragraph or Bible passage. Don't call on anyone, but ask for a volunteer, and then be patient until someone begins. Be sure to thank the person who reads aloud.

7. **Break into smaller groups occasionally.** The Grow and Worship sections provide good opportunities to break into smaller circles of 3–5 people. With a greater opportunity to talk in a small circle, people will connect more with the study, apply more quickly what they're learning, and ultimately get more out of their small group experience. A small circle also encourages a quiet person to participate and tends to minimize the effects of a more vocal or dominant member.

8. **Small circles are also helpful during prayer time.** People who are unaccustomed to praying aloud will feel more comfortable trying it with just two or three others. Also, prayer requests won't take as much time, so circles will have more time to actually pray. When you gather back with the whole group, you can have one person from each circle briefly update everyone on the prayer requests from their sub-groups. The other great aspect of sub-grouping is that it fosters leadership development. As you ask people in the group to facilitate discussion or to lead a prayer circle, it gives them a small leadership step that can build their confidence.

9. **Rotate facilitators occasionally.** You may be perfectly capable of hosting each time, but you will help others grow in their faith and gifts if you give them opportunities to host the group.

10. **One final challenge (for new or first-time hosts):** Before your first opportunity to lead, look up each of the five passages listed below. Read each one as a devotional exercise to help prepare you with a shepherd's heart. Trust us on this one. If you do this, you will be more than ready for your first meeting.

Matthew 9:36–38

"When Jesus saw the crowds, he had compassion on them, because they were harassed and helpless, like sheep without a shepherd. Then he said to his disciples, 'The harvest is plentiful but the workers are few. Ask the Lord of the harvest, therefore, to send out workers into his harvest field.'"

John 10:14–15

"I am the good shepherd; I know my sheep and my sheep know me—just as the Father knows me and I know the Father—and I lay down my life for the sheep."

1 Peter 5:2–4

"Be shepherds of God's flock that is under your care, serving as overseers—not because you must, but because you are willing, as God wants you to be; not greedy for money, but eager to serve; not lording it over those entrusted to you, but being examples to the flock. And when the Chief Shepherd appears, you will receive the crown of glory that will never fade away."

Philippians 2:1–5

"If you have any encouragement from being united with Christ, if any comfort from his love, if any fellowship with the Spirit, if any tenderness and compassion, then make my joy complete by being like-minded, having the same love, being one in spirit and purpose. Do nothing out of selfish ambition or vain conceit, but in humility consider others better than yourselves. Each of you should look not only to your own interests, but also to the interests of others. Your attitude should be the same as that of Jesus Christ."

Hebrews 10:23–25

"Let us hold unswervingly to the hope we profess, for he who promised is faithful. And let us consider how we may spur one another on toward love and good deeds. Let us not give up meeting together, as some are in the habit of doing, but let us encourage one another—and all the more as you see the Day approaching."

1 Thessalonians 2:7, 8, 11–12

"But we were gentle among you, like a mother caring for her little children. We loved you so much that we were delighted to share with you not only the Gospel of God but our lives as well, because you had become so dear to us . . . . For you know that we dealt with each of you as a father deals with his own children, encouraging, comforting and urging you to live lives worthy of God, who calls you into his kingdom and glory."

FREQUENTLY ASKED QUESTIONS

How long will this group meet?

This volume of *Inside Out Living* is six sessions long. We encourage your group to add a seventh session for a celebration. In your final session, each group member may decide if he or she desires to continue on for another study. At that time you may also want to do some informal evaluation, discuss your Group Guidelines, and decide which study you want to do next. We recommend you visit our website at www.purposedriven.com for more video-based small group studies.

Who is the host?

The host is the person who coordinates and facilitates your group meetings. In addition to a host, we encourage you to select one or more group members to lead your group discussions. Several other responsibilities can be rotated, including refreshments, prayer requests, worship, or keeping up with those who miss a meeting. Shared ownership in the group helps everybody grow.

Where do we find new group members?

Recruiting new members can be a challenge for groups, especially new groups with just a few people, or existing groups that lose a few people along the way. We encourage you to use the *Circles of Life* diagram on page 64 of this workbook to brainstorm a list of people from your workplace, church, school, neighborhood, family, and so on. Then pray for the people on each member's list. Allow each member to invite several people from their list. Some groups fear that newcomers will interrupt the intimacy that members have built over time. However, groups that welcome newcomers generally gain strength with the infusion of new blood. Remember, the next person you add just might become a friend for eternity. Logistically, groups find different ways to add members. Some groups remain permanently open, while others choose to open periodically, such as at the beginning or end of a study. If your group becomes too large for easy, face-to-face conversations, you can sub-group, forming a second discussion group in another room.

How do we handle the childcare needs in our group?

Childcare needs must be handled very carefully. This is a sensitive issue. We suggest you seek creative solutions as a group. One common solution is to have the adults meet in the living room and share the cost of a baby sitter (or two) who can be with the kids in another part of the house. Another popular option is to have one home for the kids and a second home (close by) for the adults. If desired, the adults could rotate the responsibility of providing a lesson for the kids. This last option is great with school age kids and can be a huge blessing to families.

Purpose Driven Group Guidelines

It's a good idea for every group to put words to their shared values, expectations, and commitments. Such guidelines will help you avoid unspoken agendas and unmet expectations. We recommend you discuss your guidelines during Session One in order to lay the foundation for a healthy group experience. Feel free to modify anything that does not work for your group.

We agree to the following values:

Clear Purpose   To grow healthy spiritual lives by building a healthy
                           small group community

Group Attendance   To give priority to the group meeting (call if I am
                           absent or late)

Safe Environment   To create a safe place where people can be heard
                           and feel loved (no quick answers, snap judgments,
                           or simple fixes)

Be Confidential   To keep anything that is shared strictly confidential
                           and within the group

Conflict Resolution   To avoid gossip and to immediately resolve any concerns
                           by following the principles of Matthew 18:15–17

Spiritual Health   To give group members permission to speak into my
                           life and help me live a healthy, balanced spiritual life
                           that is pleasing to God

Limit Our Freedom   To limit our freedom by not serving or consuming
                           alcohol during small group meetings or events so as
                           to avoid causing a weaker brother or sister to stumble
                           (1 Corinthians 8:1–13; Romans 14:19–21)

Welcome Newcomers   To invite friends who might benefit from this study and warmly welcome newcomers

Building Relationships   To get to know the other members of the group and pray for them regularly

Other   _____

We have also discussed and agree on the following items:

Child Care

_____

_____

Starting Time

_____

Ending Time

_____

If you haven't already done so, take a few minutes to fill out the *Small Group Calendar* on page 67.

Circles of Life—Small Group Connections

Discover who you can connect in community

Use this chart to help carry out one of the values in the *Group Guidelines*, to "Welcome Newcomers."

"Follow me and I will make you fishers of men." Matthew 4:19

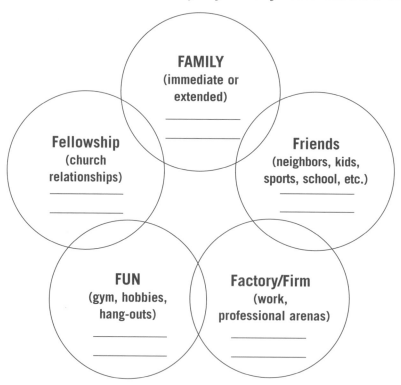

Follow this simple three-step process:

1. List 1–2 people in each circle.

2. Prayerfully select one person or couple from your list and tell your group about them.

3. Give them a call and invite them to your next meeting. Over fifty percent of those invited to a small group say, "Yes!"

Small Group Prayer and Praise Report

This is a place where you can write each other's requests for prayer. You can also make a note when God answers a prayer. Pray for each other's requests. If you're new to group prayer, it's okay to pray silently or to pray by using just one sentence: "God, please help _____ to _____ ."

DATE	PERSON	PRAYER REQUEST	PRAISE REPORT

Small Group Prayer and Praise Report

DATE	PERSON	PRAYER REQUEST	PRAISE REPORT

Small Group Calendar

Healthy groups share responsibilities and group ownership. It might take some time for this to develop. Shared ownership ensures that responsibility for the group doesn't fall to one person. Use the calendar to keep track of social events, mission projects, birthdays, or days off. Complete this calendar at your first or second meeting. Planning ahead will increase attendance and shared ownership.

DATE	LESSON	LOCATION	FACILITATOR	SNACK OR MEAL
10/22	Session 2	Steve & Laura's	Bill Jones	John & Alice

Answer Key

Session One — Matthew 5:1–3

You become known for what you are <u>against</u>.

You develop an <u>unloving heart</u>.

You develop a <u>self-righteous</u> attitude.

Jesus had a different kind of righteousness in mind, an <u>inward righteousness</u>.

Having a proper understanding of your <u>spiritual condition</u> in relationship to God.

Acknowledging my <u>spiritual bankruptcy</u>.

Fundamental characteristic of a person who is going to live a <u>kingdom life</u>.

The recognition that I am spiritually bankrupt and in <u>desperate need</u>.

This first beatitude is about a deep sense of <u>needing God</u>.

Session Two — Matthew 5:4–5

True happiness begins with acknowledging the darkness of our own sin and then responding with <u>mourning</u> and <u>repentance</u>.

Comfort comes in knowing that God <u>forgives</u> my sin.

You cannot fully appreciate the wonder of your salvation without appreciating what you have been <u>saved from</u>.

Meekness is power under <u>control</u>.

Being meek means that I no longer live for my <u>own agenda</u>.

As the children of God, his death means an <u>inheritance</u> is coming our way.

Session Three — Matthew 5:6–7

What Jesus condemns is an appetite and hunger that is for the stuff of this world rather than for <u>God himself</u>.

If you have received Christ as <u>your savior</u>, you are righteous.

This beatitude is about fueling our <u>desire and hunger</u> for that process of becoming like Jesus.

<u>Grace</u> is getting what you don't deserve. <u>Mercy</u> is not getting what you do deserve.

The expression of mercy toward others in our lives is the <u>outgrowth</u> of the mercy that we have personally received.

Happiness comes in dishing out large doses of <u>mercy</u>.

Session Four — Matthew 5:8–9

If you want to have a fulfilled life, you have to do a scan of your spiritual heart.

Loving God is first and foremost a matter of your heart and soul, not your actions and behaviors.

When you do something with pure motives, God is pleased and you are a success.

Purity of heart brings God into focus.

When Jesus talks about peacemaking, he means actively bringing people together who are estranged.

Be reconciled to God personally.

Introduce others to the peace that God offers.

Bring peace between people.

Session Five — Matthew 5:10–12

As you live like Jesus you too can expect some criticism and rejection along the way.

There is no honor in being persecuted because you are abrasive, offensive, and antagonistic.

Look up

Look forward

Look around

Session Six — Matthew 5:13–16

Accommodation

Isolation

Penetration

Understand the scope of your mission.

Rub shoulders with those you are called to influence.

Maintain your distinctiveness.

Accept that you are God's advertisement.

Live your faith openly.

DAILY QUIET TIME VERSES

As your group is studying the Sermon on the Mount, spend a couple of minutes each day reflecting on these key verses in your Daily Quiet Time.

1. John 10:10
2. Matthew 4:23–25
3. Matthew 5:1–3
4. Ecclesiastes 2:10–11
5. John 18:36–37
6. Isaiah 64:1–6
7. Matthew 5:4–5
8. John 16:8
9. Romans 3:10–12
10. Matthew 11:28–30
11. Colossians 3:12–14
12. Philippians 2:1–4
13. Ephesians 1:13–14
14. Matthew 5:6–7
15. 2 Corinthians 5:21
16. Luke 12:20–21
17. Psalm 63:8–11
18. Philippians 3:7–8
19. John 6:67–69
20. Lamentations 3:19–23
21. Matthew 5:8–9
22. Matthew 22:37
23. Matthew 15:7–9
24. Proverbs 4:23–25
25. Romans 12:14–19
26. Colossians 1:19–20
27. 2 Corinthians 5:18–20
28. Matthew 5:10–12
29. 2 Timothy 3:10–13
30. John 15:18–20
31. 1 Peter 4:15–16
32. 2 Corinthians 11:23–25
33. Acts 4:27–30
34. Hebrews 11:36–40
35. Matthew 5:13–16